LIGHTFALL & TIME

FIFTEEN SOUTHWESTERN NATIONAL PARKS

Paintings by Cynthia Bennett

Foreword by Ann Zwinger

Text by Susan Lamb

Grand Canyon Natural History Association, Grand Canyon, Arizona 86023
Northland Press, Flagstaff, Arizona 86002

FOREWORD

Cynthia Bennett's paintings portray the luminescence of the Southwest.

The light that bathes the landscape is different here. There is lots more of it and it comes in bigger packages, pouring out more candlepower, blasting out of a clarity of sky, shattering preconceived notions of what light and landscape are all about. Since there are no rolling green fields here, no lowland forests to absorb light, no humidity to blur horizons, light lasers canyon wall and mountain cliff, revealing the bare bones of the Southwest.

An Eastern art critic might describe the paintings as abstract, hard-edged, records of an artist's romantic imaginings of a non-existent world, portrayals of a fanciful display of color and shape, light and form, that do not exist in nature. Rubbish! That could be someone who has never been here, never awakened by the side of a silvery serpentine stream, never squinted at midday into shimmering quivering horizons, never watched a descending sun backlight faraway canyons and the intervening valleys glow with light. These paintings are neither imagined nor fantasy: they are the reality of the Southwest.

In the Southwest light is the genesis of color. It provides the tender peach of a cliff wall after a rain, the vulnerable colors of apricot and cream that blanch to the bone white of festoon-bedded Navajo Sandstone, or shining aubergine that evaporates to the dried blood of quartz-sparked Wingate Sandstone. In this landscape of light, mountains are as blue-gray as a juniper berry, canyon walls are as rosy as a stab of Indian paintbrush, a stream dying in the sand unbraids like platinum wires, and the sand itself changes color by the hour—mauve to gold to Naples yellow to pewter gray.

Cynthia Bennett, like most Southwesterners, is clearly addicted to light. In this book, she selects landscapes that are familiar to people who come to see what the Southwest is all about, and she has illumined these scenes with fidelity and devotion. These are paintings for the newcomer to the Southwest to savor: they tell of what makes the Southwest the place it is, a reminder of open skies and space to breathe. Every time you open this book and look into one of her paintings, it will bring back with a rush the cool damp clay smell of a river morning, or the cliff-fall of light that lasts but a moment, not even time for words, so that the image exists only in nonverbal memory and can be conveyed only in nonverbal ways.

These are also paintings for those of us who live in the Southwest to treasure, reminders that there is always a new way to see. When I rest beside a desert river or awake in a deep canyon where steep walls bound the sky, I look out into a Bennett painting and feel a flush of pleasure in the recognition. Sometimes her paintings evoke memories of forgotten images, memories strung like virga in melodious rhythms across a far mountain rim.

Such evocative views are the combined gift of one woman's understanding of time, light and place, and the perception of a Park Service charged with their care and maintenance. If you receive these landscapes as she painted them, you will feel an abiding commitment to their continuance. They document the fleeting fall of light on rock prow, the last shaft of light pooling on a mountain peak, the clarity that comes from a sanctity of sky. They record the glories of today we cherish and protect so that we may enjoy them for all our tomorrows.

Ann Zwinger

Colorado Springs
1986

ARCHES NATIONAL PARK

These colors are painful and intense.
We travel through a kind of light which brightens
the rocks and the plants and the sky,
all in the same way—a brilliant glaze of light.

C.B.

Arches occur in long, stone *fins* which are ridges remaining between deep cracks in the sandstone. Caused by subterranean bulging and collapse, the cracks have weathered and widened.

There is so much bare red rock here, hard and stark against the blue sky. Yet it is dissolving steadily over the years as rain and groundwater percolate through it. Freezing winters pry whole flakes away, releasing the pressures under which the rock was formed, spalling off more stone until the last, delicate whimsies of the earth are exposed briefly in geologic time, soon to crumble themselves.

Red iron oxides glaze the sand which makes up this rock. When the sandstone disintegrates, the rust stain wears away and the sand is pale again.

In Salt Valley, wind has accumulated sand and soil enough to support a grassland. *Galleta*, dropseed, and Indian ricegrass are briefly a green background in spring. Then, acres of coral globemallow bloom, closer in color to the red rock than any other flower. Smooth cones of harvester anthills, shingled with glinting quartz grains, lie within sterile, ten-foot circles the ants have denuded of all plantlife. In the soft sand of the valley, lizard and beetle tracks describe flourishes accented with perfect circles drawn by the tips of wind-whipped grass.

BRYCE CANYON NATIONAL PARK

At Yovimpa Point: a limber pine, spruce, fir,
bristlecone pine and juniper all growing
in one clump. Rainbows every day;
a meringue feeling to the stone shapes. Color and
texture and atmospheric phenomena
are all speeded up and tumbling over each other.

C.B.

Gazing eastward from the brink of the Paunsaugunt Plateau, the eye encounters a most curious geologic spectacle. The rows and bundles of B*ryce Canyon*'s tall stone pillars mark a dramatic transition from highland to plain in a baffling array of ridges and clefts. Talus ramparts bolster the bases of precipitous rock stockades. Bryce is not a canyon, but rather, an edge of high country overlooking the Paria River valley.

The soft rim rock has been shaped by weathering and gravity. Deposited by a Paleocene lake system, it was jointed by the stresses of an uplift which began millions of years ago and may still be going on. Along these joints the rock is vulnerable to erosion by frost and roots wedging its particles apart, by chemical breakdown, and by wind and water. Harder rock, slower to succumb to these forces, becomes cap rock and protruding ledges. Gravity tugs at loosened pebbles and sorts them on the way to their angles of repose, so that heavier material is deposited farthest down and the lightest tends to be near the top.

At sunset, edges of the intricate profiles of these stone totems are gilded. An uncanny infantry stands immobile, imperceptibly melting through the centuries.

CANYONLANDS NATIONAL PARK

The land is quiet, but it is not the quiet of silence:
the place is fully inhabited.
There are complicated, labyrinthine distances,
and three-hundred and sixty degrees
of storms. After the rain, everything shines.

C.B.

The essence of the Colorado Plateau is distilled in the *Canyonlands*. Here, the Green and the Colorado rivers converge and thunder into Cataract Canyon. Their deep, twisting channels draw the water of countless seasonal tributaries, which cut drainages into the plateau, ceaselessly gnawing at its edges.

Deep underground, in beds half-a-mile thick, salt has influenced this landscape, too. Unstable when overburdened with extensive deposits, the salt has been squeezed from one place to another. In the north, its upwelling once pushed the surface above it into a dome. Erosion then worried away the cap of this mound and scooped out the softer exposed rock, resulting in a mile-wide bowl now known as Upheaval Dome. By contrast, in the Needles area, the buried salt has been dissolved by underground water. The overlying sandstone blocks have sunk into long canyons, called grabens.

The complex topography of Canyonlands serves sometimes as a corridor, but more often as a barrier to most animals and plants which live here. The birds are an exception. During the day, droll, gleaming ravens flap slowly by, their wingbeats audible in the still air. The red-tailed hawk hovers high overhead, ready to drop like a stone on its prey. The hawk's piercing shriek is arresting as it echoes through these canyon walls, a sharp contrast to the chickadees' scratchy, common refrain.

CEDAR BREAKS NATIONAL MONUMENT

There is a great sensation of height to the pillars and "hoodoos" of the Wasatch Limestone. Trees, themselves weathered to the essence, provide emphatic touches on all of the edges.

C.B.

The thin, high air of *Cedar Breaks* is sharpened by the scent of pine and fir. Curmudgeonly red squirrels chatter imperiously at intruders. Their world is a forest of mixed conifers, oaks, and aspens, broken by alpine meadows brimming with wildflowers.

Pikas, furry and chubby, busy themselves in summer, harvesting grasses and strewing them over rocks to dry for winter provisions. They peep around boulders, watching for predators, their sudden, peremptory squeaks bouncing from their hiding places. Less shy, chipmunks and marmots are often seen during the day.

Abruptly, one encounters the brink of a westward-facing escarpment which plunges more than 2000 feet. Arcing in a ten-square-mile bite out of the western rim of the Markagunt Plateau, it is smaller sister to Bryce Canyon. Cedar Breaks is inaccessible to man, a maze complicated by ravines and ridges of vivid red, buff, and ochre limestone.

The bristlecone pine lives here. Strange that the oldest living individuals on earth should be those which must survive the most daunting conditions. Blasted by wind, subjected to freezing and unshielded from the glaring sun, deprived of moisture and soil, they endure the most, yet endure the longest. The bristlecone, infinitely tolerant of adversity, is virtually indomitable.

GLEN CANYON NATIONAL RECREATION AREA

From the tip of the Paria Plateau, the river below
flashes down to Lees Ferry and into
the Colorado. There is lightning over a nearby drift
of wind-blown coral sand.
Soon, thunder from the Echo Cliffs.

C.B.

The bright sky, honey-colored stone, and clear blue water of *Glen Canyon* seem to be the whole world at first, as in some primeval creation story. Gradually, details emerge from this first impression of fathomless reservoir and soaring sandstone. The water is dotted with ducks and coots. It mirrors perfectly the dark streaks of desert varnish and the high, shallow arches of the cliffs. The immense sky is sometimes host to odd-shaped clouds, and can darken and divide with powerful thunderstorms.

Water laps at the walls of an infinite number of tight, twisting side canyons, ripples scattering reflected light into the shadows. Exploring stone ledges and alcoves, a person can stride quickly up dry slickrock in spite of apparently impossible inclines, to find forgotten petroglyphs and seepspring nooks of maidenhair fern and golden columbine.

Afternoon brings the raspy chattering of swifts as they swoop about in pursuit of insects. The water's surface plinks and sparkles with leaping fish. And then at night, though occasionally broken by the wail of a coyote, the silence of Glen Canyon is profound. One can almost hear the stars falling from the glittering sky.

Rain in the night, potholes brimming
on the rim, the river running brown, red, pink,
orange, purple and vermilion—
a real river for awhile.

C.B.

Grand Canyon drops away a mile below one's feet to the river, and disappears on either side into the lilac reaches of its nearly 300-mile length. The abyss, the formidable space itself, is a sentient presence. It provokes many to contemplate time and change, beauty and power, life and spirit.

Beginning in the classic, high canyon country and ending on the edge of the Colorado Plateau, it also teaches principles of the natural world. It illustrates the processes of the earth: deposition, uplift, and erosion. In a patchwork of environments, shading from cool rim forest through desert to river, it demonstrates the roles of temperature, slope, moisture, and soil.

But in encountering this place, one also feels very much in the present, of the moment. The intense sunlight, air pungent with sage, and steepness of canyon trails bedazzle the hiker. River voyagers are carried, ecstatic, by the whirling water rushing through the towering gorge. And those who sit on the rim, enveloped in the warm, cliffrose-scented afternoon, delight in the iridescent, violet-green swallows dipping and soaring as shadows lengthen into the magnificence of sunset over Grand Canyon.

Below the dam, Lake Mohave backs
into caves and side canyons and into the pools of
hot springs. There are cliff swallows
and nests, cormorants, snowy egrets, Canada geese
and a million other birds,
and desert bighorn sheep disguised as rocks
on the slopes above.

C.B.

Cynthia Bennett

Lake Mead National Recreation Area is actually two lakes, Mead and Mohave, created by dams on the Colorado River. They partly inundate the bed of a late Pleistocene lake, Chemehuevi. That lake would have been the result of a natural dam, perhaps a landslide or a lava flow. Eventually, the river conquered this obstacle and flowed again to the Gulf of California.

Lake Mohave fills a valley in the geologic province known as "basin and range." Here, the earth's surface is bulging from pressures generated in the mantle below. Rifting apart, the crust has broken into blocks. In the process, these fault blocks have tilted and dropped, and their upper edges form the parallel north-south mountain ranges characteristic of the area.

Ten thousand years ago, people adapted to the forbidding conditions along the dry washes. Living on wild plants and small game, they roamed with the seasons, hardly touching the land. Eventually, they settled in pueblos, but mysteriously departed nine centuries ago. Their place was taken by nomadic ancestors of the Paiutes, living in the old hunter-gatherer way. These people watched the world closely, aware of its every sound, scent, and movement.

In the 1800s, the Paiutes were joined by determined pioneers who struggled tenaciously to survive. Today, the dam provides abundant power and water. However temporarily, man dominates nature in this place for the first time.

NATURAL BRIDGES NATIONAL MONUMENT

"White Canyon"—white stone,
even white lichen on the stone—is lovely in its
tinyness: pothole gardens in bloom,
toy forests on the caprock, bonsai trees on the faces
of cliffs. Every aspect of life here
is miniature and intimate.

C.B.

In this once flat place, streams cut their beds in big, looping meanders, isolating tongues of rock. Incessant scouring by the turbid water has worn right through these at their bases, creating *Natural Bridges*.

The scarce, lumpy patches of soil found in this environment are blackened by a lifeless-looking crust. Nothing could appear less significant. But this layer of cryptogams forms a base in which other, larger plants may grow. A symbiotic community composed of mosses and lichens, *Cryptogamia* ("hidden wedlock") cloaks the meager soil in a spongy blanket which soaks up and retains any moisture. Without cryptogams, the soil would wash or blow away, leaving bare slickrock. Where a footpath passes through an area of cryptogams, the soil on either side of the trail is lofted into banks. The path itself is continually eroding away, as footsteps destroy these organisms.

Shaggy junipers, riddled with sapsucker holes, are the dominant trees. Their twisted forms can survive on less water than any others. The Douglas-firs just under the brinks of shady cliffs, the cottonwoods and willows on the riverbanks on the canyon floor, and even the pinyon pines are outnumbered. Juniper leaves are tiny and expose a minimum of surface area to evaporation since they overlap like fishscales and have a waxy coating. The trees' roots probe into cracks in the rock for moisture. Periodically a juniper is covered with powder blue or coppery "berries," which are really a type of cone. The ever-hungry coyote may occasionally be seen, paws up on a juniper trunk, making a meal of these dubious delicacies.

We have a smoky fire—the kind
that steams rather than brightens. In the desert
night, its ash (as well as blowing dust)
becomes a permanent part of each person. We feel
enshrined by the desert.

C.B.

To spend a morning in *Organ Pipe Cactus National Monument* is to begin a fascination with the Sonoran Desert. Cactuses, one of nature's experiments in defying dryness and heat, delight and mystify with their strange beauty. Infinitely diverse, they are believed to be very young, evolutionarily.

Surprisingly, here almost all growing things reach up towards the shimmering sun. There is no soft, drooping foliage. Even the ribs of saguaro skeletons point stiffly, and sotol stalks stand rigid.

Rain brings an instant response from everything in the desert. Ocotillo, many-branched candelabra of thorny stems fifteen feet high, are unable to store water. They bear leaves only after rain falls, and burst into flame-red blossoms in the moist spring. The leaves of the creosote bush, which curl up to conserve water in the sunshine, unfurl during showers to release a piquant scent.

It is very different down in the washes, which froth with muddy water during rainstorms. Many plants thrive here, providing food and shelter for more wildlife than the parched slopes above. In the sandy beds of washes, coyotes dig shallow wells which are then visited by many other creatures, even swarms of bees.

It is very quiet in midday, with only the occasional low scolding of the cactus wren. When the wind gusts through the sagebrush, its sound is like that of the ocean. Cool evenings come early from fall through spring, bringing sunsets brilliant with the rubies and vermilions of dust-laden air.

The colors here are grays: black-and-white-grays,
blue-grays, complementary-colors-grays.
The color washes over the hills and gives truth
to the scenery as a "painted" desert.

C.B.

Desolate yet lovely, *Petrified Forest* expresses the changeable nature of our earth. Though it is now an almost lunar terrain, erosion of the soft earth has revealed the late Triassic of 200 million years ago—a swamp of braided streams, huge trees, ferns and enormous reptiles. In slanted layers of muted rose, lavender, cream, and brown are found the fossils of a world that lasted 30 million years.

Our footsteps leave hardly a trace on the badlands. Scattered among the mudcracks are the jewels of the Painted Desert: fragments of petrified wood in deep, glassy colors of ruby, amethyst, jet, and amber. The structure of ancient wood can be seen in the larger pieces, where tree-ring patterns radiate in haloes of color.

The familiar shrubs—yucca, sagebrush, and Mormon tea—brightened by the blooms of salmon globemallow and blue lupine, are utterly different from the ferns and lush seed plants of a humid earlier world. The dissolving slopes offer a poor foothold, and many of the plants which grow here now are in the flat washes.

Intriguing figures chipped into the black varnish of tumbled sandstone slabs bring alive the mystery and imagination of those people who lived here a thousand years ago. But few venture into the Painted Desert wilderness now. Grasshoppers clatter in bounds across a lonely, eerie landscape of buttes, twisting arroyos, and fallen stone trees.

The year has been wet and the cactus are filled with
water, their pleats smoothed out.
It is storming now: a big canyon wind combed by
saguaro spines sounds like
a freight train. Later, everything turns green.

C.B.

Saguaro National Monument protects a forest of remarkable beings. Symbols of the desert Southwest, saguaro cactus are enormous, pleated stems stretching up 40 feet or more. Their wide-ranging, shallow roots anchor strong skeletons inside a mass of tissue which, nonetheless, sways gently in the breeze.

Saguaros grow most favorably on the characteristic sloping fans—*bajadas*—of dirt and rock spread below parent fault-block mountains. As water drains quickly through the thin *bajada* soil, the saguaro's roots engorge the cactus, expanding its accordion folds. Then, protected by its waxy skin, the saguaro survives the stunning heat of summer by drawing moisture from its own pulp and energy from the sunlight spilling so relentlessly over it. Often sheltered by "nurse" palo verde for their first half-century of life, slow growing saguaro can reach a great age, their branches sheltering huge raptor nests in their turn.

A person can walk swiftly over the packed earth, free in seemingly endless space and light. But one soon learns not to barge insensibly through the desert. Rather, a cautious path, as through an enchanted garden, avoids the catclaw acacia whose delicate leaves conceal entangling thorns. Yellow, bristling chunks of teddybear cholla feast on the shoes and trouserlegs of the unwary, although wrens and curved-bill thrashers raise their young among the branches, and packrats build fabulous palaces of the heaped-up stems.

Movement from a hole high in a saguaro catches the eye—a gilded flicker slips out and snaps away across the desert, revealing yellow underwings. Jackrabbits suddenly bolt from brittlebush almost underfoot, and leap crashing away through the scrub. In the evening, roosting quail, startled by the sound of footsteps, burst up from the mesquite trees with a tremendous racket. And at night the cactus open their soft blooms in anticipation of the insects which move about only in the cool, dark air.

SUNSET CRATER NATIONAL MONUMENT

Hundreds of volcanic cones make up the cinder hills,
each dusted by wind until all
particles are settled according to size. The forest is
spare, vegetation not covering,
but giving a punch of color to the cones.

C.B.

In this region of incomprehensible geologic time spans, the freshness of the landform *Sunset Crater* is striking. Fairest for its symmetry and rosy-orange summit, Sunset Crater is youngest in a field of hundreds of volcanic cinder cones, cousins to the spectacular San Francisco Peaks.

Seeing it serene now, in summer rising above meadows of sunflowers, in winter above sparkling snowfields, it is difficult to imagine Sunset Crater's beginning. Two hundred years of earthquakes, hails of ash, alternating explosions of cinders and outpourings of molten rock ten times the temperature of boiling water gradually built the cone, then diminished until just vapors issued from its hollows. These vapors tinged the crown with oxidized minerals, which glow yet again in the long, low rays of the setting sun each day.

At first glance, the lava flows appear raw and unweathered by the nine centuries since their creation. Frozen in motion, jagged slabs of porous crust were jumbled at all angles from the movement of underlying rock that was slower to harden so long ago. On closer look, the lichen one sees ornamenting the rough black rock, in patches of yellow, gold, and lime green, must have taken most of those nine centuries to grow there. Mature ponderosa pine grow out of the lava flow, too. Weathering is taking place after all, and one day the landscape will no longer tell the story of its creation so dramatically.

TUZIGOOT NATIONAL MONUMENT

Looking up at the ruin with Mingus Mountain
behind—a large hawk lands near.
There are ducks. People living at Tuzigoot went in
and out through hatches in the roof.
You could open the ceiling to the birds and the sky.

C.B.

Squawks of great blue herons stalking the marsh waft up to the summit of *Tuzigoot*. Below, on the other side of the hill, kingfishers swoop among the sycamores and cottonwoods lining the Verde River as it meanders through its fertile terraces.

During the catastrophic drought of 800 years ago, many farmers of the Southwest desperately sought dependable sources of water. From the north, Sinagua came to the Verde Valley and lived in harmony with those already here. On the crest of this ridge, they built an imposing, two-storied town. The ruined walls of its 77 rooms lie on the hilltop like a broken honeycomb.

The valley drew more and more others, refugees probably from places with no rivers to water their crops. Eventually, it is believed, every bit of farmland here was in use, and many stone cities grew up within sight of one another. A vigorous way of life developed at this crossroads of cultures.

Then, as in so many other parts of the Southwest before, these towns were suddenly abandoned. Nothing archaeologists can find explains exactly why. The land might have been exhausted; a plague may have struck. Perhaps enemies appeared on the horizon; perhaps the people became enemies to one another. The people of Tuzigoot live on, it is thought, in the pueblos of today.

Drippings from snow melt are everywhere.
The trees struggle up from rocks.
People lived in shadows, under overhangs, in cracks
here. Life cannot have been easy.
But there would have been firewood, game meat and
grains. There would have been children
sounds and laughter.

C.B.

The mood of *Walnut Canyon*, home of the prehistoric Sinagua, is one of tranquility. It is an oasis of forest and stream, with cozy rooms tucked under ledges partway down the canyon walls. Blackened ceilings bring to mind the days when Sinagua people built their cooking fires here. In the early morning, the chirp and flutter of many birds echo the liveliness of Walnut Canyon when its 300 rooms were home to an extraordinary people.

A rich variety of plants and animals were once sources of food, clothing, fuel, or implements for these self-sufficient people. Our modern alarm at the evident hardships of primitive life is mocked by the exuberant decoration of the most commonplace Sinagua goods. Clay pots did not hold their contents any better for having been elaborately painted. Only the maker or wearer of sandals intricately woven in colored patterns would have been aware of how pretty the soles of their shoes were. Those were the kind of people, stone-age people, to whom such details mattered. They spent many hours patiently crafting lovely things with which to surround themselves.

The narrow canyon and bare stone walls suggest a confined world, but turquoise, cotton, and seashells found among those ruins tell us of lives linked by trade and travel to far-off canyons, deserts, and oceans.

ZION NATIONAL PARK

The lines of buttes and temples and mesas
are clear when seen against the light. In the late
afternoon and early morning
the canyon is still surrounding, but its forms
become separate and begin to be understandable.

C.B.

One hundred sixty million years ago, a vast desert covered the area that now includes *Zion*. Howling winds blew fine layers of sand into mountainous dunes, which coursed across the land in waves. The fickle winds of this remote past shifted often, and more dunes trending in different directions accumulated over the earlier ones; chemicals from later deposits percolated down and fossilized their graceful curves.

The Virgin River's north fork emerges into the broad reaches of Zion Canyon from its steep-walled passage through the Narrows. It undercuts the walls of its channel which then collapse, revealing the sweeping patterns of the ancient dunes.

The river perpetually cools and waters the canyon floor. Broad-leaved trees and many birds thrive here. Shady grottoes, luxuriant with ferns, velvety mosses, and crimson monkeyflower, are the home of *Petrophysa zionis*, a tiny snail found nowhere else in the world.

Early spring flowers of pink, lavender, and blue emerge on the plateau as winter's snows are melting. Their fragile colors fade quickly when the days turn warm and dry. Then the torrential "monsoons" hammer the Colorado Plateau in July and August. Yellow and orange members of *Compositae*, the sunflower family, now dominate, foretelling the golden leaves of autumn to come.

photo by Sue Bennett

The canyons and mesas and peaks of the Southwest have been an inspiration to Cynthia Bennett for twenty years. Her characteristic simplicity of line and extraordinary use of color and light have earned for her paintings the distinction of immediate recognition.

Born in Ohio, Bennett grew up in Hawaii. She came to Arizona in 1966 and lived in Grand Canyon National Park until she moved to Sedona in 1976 to work full time as a painter. She is a graduate of Northern Arizona University.

"I first became interested in painting the Southwest in 1966 in the Lower Grand Canyon. It was night. The cliffs were purple, a moon topped the rims and yes, a coyote bawled and squalled for the sheer enjoyment of it. I knew that my help came from the hills and I would always be painting here."

Each Cynthia Bennett canvas is the drama of a story never told but oft remembered. Her canyons and mountain stretches inspire awe, but speak of intimacy; her rivers electrify. The fifteen paintings of LIGHTFALL & TIME typify this Cynthia Bennett mystique.

To the friends who have helped me, I am grateful. Deep thanks are especially due to: Tom and Jane Aderhold, Paul Babbitt Jr., Gordon Barnett, Peter Bennett, Jeff Christensen, Gary Ladd, Lucinda Navarre, David Platt, Susan Silberberg-Peirce, and Bob Young. And to Ann Zwinger, whose words and drawings have been a constant source of stimulation and joy.

This book is for Christie and Martha and Denny.

Edited by Sandra Scott
Designed by Christina Watkins
Typeset in Novarese and Helvetica by Typesmith, Inc.
Printed by Northland Press

Library of Congress Number 86-81412

ISBN 0-87358-425-2 (*paperback*)
ISBN 0-87358-426-0 (*hardbound*)